TALKING WITH TREES

poems
by **LUCIA COPPOLA**

Talking With Trees

For Michael and Sam

« Marion s'y promène le long de son jardin
Le long de son jardin sur les bords de la France,
Le long de son jardin sur les bords de l'eau… »

(Malicorne)

"Marion goes walking in her garden
walks in her garden by the shores of France
in her garden she goes walking down by the waterside"

TALKING WITH TREES

Table of Contents:

Part I: Walking

Part II: In The Garden

Part III: By the Waterside

TALKING WITH TREES

INTRODUCTION:

These verse and prose poems were written between 2009 and 2010 in what was initially a spiritual exploration. As I was writing, nature increasingly became my guide. I am grateful for the rose, apricot, apple, and maple trees I regularly saw outside my window each day.

I am also grateful to my family for their love and support, my dear friend, poet, playwright, and novelist M.Z. Ribalow for his encouragement, my brother Bruno Coppola, for the photo of the birds on the lake and his insightful comments, as well as Francis Massart for his kind and thoughtful presence throughout my first drafts and most of the photos shown here. Many thanks to Jamie Nix, editor at Plants & Poetry, for helping me bring this project to fruition.

Some of these pieces were read in earlier versions on the New York Clocktower Radio, New River Writers series: "Rocks", "The Bridge" and "Roses". Some have been published in print form: "Riddle" in The Parliament Literary Journal, "Secret Gardens" in the Plants and Poetry Anthology, "Rocks" and "The Clearing" in Soul-Lit and "The Oak Tree" and "The Cedar Tree" in the Vita Brevis Anthology III.

"Talking With Trees" is conceived as an arc that extends over a specific time and place - what I call here my "garden."

PART I

WALKING

THE NEED FOR FIRE

There's a pale glow of sunlight
where the morning comes
through the panes
across the floor beams shining
shadows of foliage from outside projecting — still
the smell of coffee and the residual sound
of an alarm clock
that rang just minutes ago.

Pieces of last night's Risk game
are scattered
One soldier is standing
one is down
and several are turned eastwards
for a future encampment
or battle... who knows?
This is a place of quiet
with just the faint sound
of Cornflakes crunching
and everything is paused
with the day only now to begin.

Driving to school
driving to work
the radio plays reggae.
There's fog on the windshield, a chill in the air
and not much wind though there's a sense of the flow.
Time is master here as car doors
get opened and shut

as the schoolbag gets left behind
and the motor's already running
and we're down the street and oh no...
the bag's in the car after all...

A brief sigh lingers
with the frost and the fog
the faint smell of plastic and a hint of early snow
as forward we charge with the thump in our beat
since we know the words to the song
and we sing along...
You win when you get to the right destination.
There's relief when you get there on time.

Time for work, time for play
where a circle is cast
and our words like smooth stones
move from one to the other with soft,
whispered flow.
No jagged edges here
but the texture of our contingency
holding one another's presence
like a pebble
like an empty space, coveting that place
where fortune reveals that what we need most
is simply the dream of this day together.

To go back home — to sit, to lie down
to stand up only thinking
it's time to cast a glance
however quick at the feeling
as if holding it in the palm of a hand
like soft amber —
the surface of skin
warm from light in embers glowing
with the hint of a wish,
with the hint of despair
and a nod to what needs
to be known.

Is the refrigerator filled?
Is there mail?
Would going away for spring break
be extravagant?
Or maybe we should have another child,
a puppy, more goldfish...a mouse?
However delicate, however small
however tricky
the pumpkin needs carving now —
tricky the balance of dusk with dawn.
Whatever the situation may be
it begins at this most peaceful place
of kindling — even in
the dimness
of the light.

ROCKS

If you listen to them carefully
 you may hear the most extraordinary things.

They need to be coaxed into it
and arranged in particular ways
but usually they manage all by themselves.
They only seem dumb because they're not good movers
though they vibrate continuously.

***

Bones and branches are similar but less solid
marrowed with light as opposed to reflecting it.
 The language is more like living dance
than some arcane, forgotten chant.

This is why roots of trees creep under rocks
and fingers and toes into sand.
The melody finds harmony with its bass.

Sifting through the silt by the banks of a river
we may find gold, but it takes
a bit of leverage, patience and concentration.
The mechanical gesture requires
more alchemy
than good luck.

Once I found a roundish green rock
in the shallow current of a stream.
It was beautifully polished and resembled a Buddha.
It had a little cave for a mouth that chanted "Om"
and in that "Om" there was a place
that smelled of the earth and of springtime,

so I lay down in that green until the fall of the night,

watched a firefly nearby and saw the iridescent
sparks of its wings present as stars in the sky.
In that moment the stars were a choir
singing "halleluia" up above
and the firefly, a fairy dancing here below.

I weighed the possibility they might be
pretending what they're not —
that the star may be nothing
but a clump of dust and the firefly, a bug.
Or maybe they're exactly what they
would have us believe, or maybe a mixture of both.

These are the thoughts I lay down in the grass next to me.
Then I fell asleep and dreamed.
Without alchemy dreams vanish into air.
But if we look, we'll find a color, a smell, a certain walk
or laugh or smile. Hands, eyes and the texture of skin
are not forgotten but etched into oneself. They're proof
that nothing is illusory about the enchantment of a rock.

***

The crypt, the well, the church
atop a mountain suspended in the sky — rocks
the very substance of our dreams, real as the empty howl of night.
From ashes and dust, they rumble and mumble and roar —
crystalline forms of varying densities.

Listen and you may hear them!
From out of the dust

they say, "Amen".

THE CLEARING

Our boots are clumped with mud and on our backs
we carry little wings. We gather for the circle dance
and sprouting roots we take hands in the round.

But it's when the dance takes off that the journey really begins
with time reeling, thumping, treading towards the taking off
of us with our wings into the air. Pirouetting with the beat,
we skip with the glide, the float and pause as further down
the earth has become a refrain — point of stillness, darker
with a more introspective vibrancy —
then silence,
briefly pausing
before the next upbeat and rest.

The great adventure takes place in the air,
where the song is best sung
with lyrics implying questions about
what may be the next stopping off.
How long for each moment
to weave itself like a tale of enchantment
into that thing that laughs,
and sighs and weeps at night?

Rituals of carnage — rituals of peace.
This moment exists despite the possibility
that severed heads may be on maypoles not so far away.

We choose to be the antidote to the lynching mobs --
to the townsfolk that taunt, torture, tease,
and have the audacity to cast shadows.
To them we answer stomping down upon the darkness
as our laughter winds its way
past dusk towards dawn,
echoing between the branle and the gigue.
Once again we hold hands
knowing never to forget.

Dearly we pay for decisions we make
and dearly we pray. We stutter and we kiss.
Does the realization of who we are now
bring with it the gentleness of grace? Perhaps....
At least the sun above and the water below will have touched
as again and again the circle is cast, and again we go round.
How far we are then
from those coldest of cold winter nights.

Sweet pilgrimage with children, elders
and songs with truest meanings.
Sweet legs, feet, fingers that grasp
this golden rule of our entwinement.
Our sweat glistens like clouds that gather
then stream down with rain.
For in this place the circle of light beckons
with each rise and fall.
Quiet like the empyrean echo of a bagpipe —

a breath that billows and spirals round a core,

as rhythm calls to gather

rhythm calls to scatter —

gather and scatter,

then follows its way around again

and back to a circular pause.

THE OAK TREE

Not the truth —
just a lens — a spectrum of possibilities
amidst the rollicking leaves when going there along
what looks like a trail, though we usually just amble
through shafts and flickers of light toward the oak
which is as close as we ever get to a destination
with no indication but the veil of sunlight, fog or rain
shared with a friend — a tree, a rock, a stump in the sun
for a brief stop in winter and with the fall of night

Not the way —
just a feeling — a mood that hovers like a film
and alters color depending on how we do the trip — bicycles,
no cars or motorcycles, no virtual screens.
The simplest way is on foot — a transfer of weight
and an inclination forwards

And a point of view amongst pinecones
and treasures that exult in their own serendipity
like the big white heart we found painted on a tree trunk
when we had just been talking about love
And cleaning up litter on the way —
a chance to bring some air to the earth
as we clear the ground
for a crow to land and stare cross-eyed at us saying
whatever crows say

And the thrill of reading signs,
avoiding holes and bramble
that creep up unforeseen and badger about uncertainty,

survival, being upside down and picking nettles out of hair —
the relief of getting past parasites, the scorn of others,
prowlers at night

Not a religion —

just a tree — a companion we look in on,
an elder of the community and witness to our words — a tree
that filters the daily din and bids us to come and curl up
to breathe, to lean steadfast into day
with a sense of destination,
with roots like arms that extend all around
so we want to linger
and travel back again to where

a squirrel passes,
acorns stuffed into its little cheeks, an owl hoots
with the fall of the night, a crow lands with urgency and says...
How do you spell it?

C-A-W —

Yes, double U

one U that journeys and one U that stays

One U that stays by the old oak

THE BRIDGE

Near my house there's a bridge
It goes over a lake

It's really more like a swamp, but I like to think of it as a lake
There's some fishing there, picnics and Sunday walkers

It's the place where my children learned to ride bikes, fly kites
and skid pebbles across the water's surface

It's a place to do nothing

The legend is that a lady once lived in this lake. She had a magic
sword which she gave to a man passing by. He carried both the sword and
the lady far away with him, and during that time she learned to walk. Being
a creature of the lake, at first she could only just swim and the walking came
slowly with time.

One day when they'd gone far away, the man disappeared. By then
the lady had forgotten how to swim and got stuck on land. Also by then she
had children who were born with feet but not fins.

##

It seems that now several years later she crosses the bridge regularly, but
always by night as the crossing over is perilous and the day filled with a
thousand other things to be done. She knows it's better after sunset when no
one can see her and with a lantern because of all the fog at night.

The real difficulty is that having forgotten how to swim, should she fall
into the lake she may drown. She prefers to go by night and believes that if she
had to, she would somehow fly. So deep is her conviction that the vestiges of
her fins have become tiny wings. But only by night. She doesn't give much

thought to the risk she takes by doing what she does. She crosses the bridge to gather food for her family — not the food that we eat but all of what else we need to stay alive.

She digs down in silt and mud
scratches roots for dance and tunes
words and sometimes flowers that appear
in clusters with the moon
when she arrives with haste to survive
and forages for what she holds dear
with neither time to tarry
nor even to feel fear

She carries her lantern, wears warm clothes, and keeps a sharp eye all around her. Should she need to, she will fly. She has no choice as there's only the bridge, her feet, and something like wings. Nobody's ever seen her there, but the legend has yielded much speculation on the part of the townspeople. Occasionally we talk about her by the lake with the bridge on days when there's nothing to do.

We talk about the lady of the lake and also the dangers of the forest. We say she knows more about these things than she'd ever be willing to tell any of us for fear of being called mad -- after all, she was the one that had the sword to begin with.

We talk about how although she now shops for groceries at the supermarket like the rest of us, she continues to cross over the bridge by night. Some people even make jokes about her falling into the lake with the fire department rescue team fishing her out at dawn. I've noticed they tend not to think of the lady of the lake in terms of her magic, but more as an oddity -- a weirdo flailing her arms about, gasping for breath, torn up clothes and hair embedded with slime.

The joking always seems to appear as proof that the magic of our dreams is somehow a threat and that we're probably better off sitting at home at night, not asking too many questions in front of the T.V.

# #

But there are some of us that find comfort in the thought that should the bridge fall down she might be our only last hope, with those wings that she seems to have managed somehow to invent. We talk about the prospect of having feet and fins and wings ourselves — about the importance of not forgetting how to swim, about how we too once crawled out of the slime.

We consider the possibility that with human evolution
bridges may one day become obsolete.

And we talk about how we may feel
on that day in this world by the lake

With no lady to help us
and no bridge to cross over.

PART II

IN THE GARDEN

RIDDLE

There are two chipped and weathered stone figures
on the steps of this sculpture garden near where I live.
They look like cherubs guarding a gate
and though cold to the touch they seem soft and round
with eyes that tell of a flame that's within.
One has the gentle look of innocence and the other a harsh glare.
Were they to speak, I guess the first one would gurgle
and the second would narrow its eyes, hiss, and stare.

The grassy part of the lawn with the well-spaced sculptures
invites me to do a little ambling. I look lingeringly upon
the curious forms and nameplates hidden
between eyelets, bluebells, daisies, and whatnots. There's
"Rhinoceros – Wood," "Circe – Stone," "Mother – Walls"
an amusing steel dot on a line– "Dialogue at 45° on the Hypotenuse".
The gibberish is bemusing, so I move along with my own point of view.
"Abstract Noir" reflects on a pool with a golden glow
and looks like angel wings emerging from below.

I suppose Heaven and Hell must be here in this place
where the paths are so straight and perplexing.
And I wonder who first put the cherubs there?
I wonder why I even care - though one thing is certain:
This is a place of delicate crafting –
of worms that churn soil cavorting with bees that stir air
of bronze hippos designing space with a correlated square
of looking at what can't be by looking seen – things
like angels that pass, the tease and tap of wings.

Now I see them, now I don't. I'm tempted to call them by names
but I'm not sure it suits them as they prefer to be secret
and if you do count them you'll always find more and more.
Each one, like numbers, tends to invoke all the rest
so I'm left speaking of relationships: guardian,
messenger, score-keeper, choir...

And there are two of them here where I stand by the gate.
Having guessed what they are, should they speak
I may guess what they say.
But they won't speak except in riddles or tongues,
or on a special day.
Doers as opposed to talkers, they're busy all the time.
They put their buzzers on mute, shift shapes, change winds.
Just now I can't help but wonder at how well
they're providing perspective.

MAPS

There are all kinds of them: the ones we keep folded up in the car

and never look at

and those from grade school that get transported by animals —

turtles, I recall

those that say if you go too far you'll fall off the edge of the world,
that make you think you're going East to India
when actually it's to the other side,
and then lots and lots of new maps need to be made
with directions for Heaven and Hell, the invisible, the obvious,
timelines of the past, crystal balls for the future, right now.
Whether round, flat, linear, photographed by satellite or drawn
with a stick in the sand, they all try to show a picture of how it is.
It helps if they come with a key.

Today we're leaving the house
with skateboards, bathing suits, sandwiches —

We could do this day with our eyes closed, except that the sky
is clear and there are rhododendrons all over the place
the most beautiful fuchsia that I've ever seen.
They're there as I take out my car keys and drive past the other houses
and there as I remember events with different shades of familiarity —
dinners, block parties, the throwing of wayward soccer balls over fences,
echoes of laughter, cries of pain, conversations in the yard,
the perpetual opening and closing of doors. These many things
are recorded in our thoughts over time.

And the rhododendrons are there as we sit on the grass.
They nod at the odd four-leaf clover and the dandelion for a wish,
and look on as we drive back home past the park, the school,
the grocer, the graveyard and church, and then again once we arrive
at home wondering how long does the blossoming last?
Does this particular map inform us about destiny or fate?
Or does it just speak of the day? A map of the day, or more specifically
of moments that flash forth sideways, sassy like lipstick
and painted toenails, leaving an impression, seductive and bold.

Today is a day of fuchsia
with rhododendrons all over the place.
Each blossom is specific to itself
just as each of us dwells here
with ancestries from far away:
China, Siberia, the Alps.
We are in this place today,
and the radiant petals of this flower
are effusive with color from the sun.

This is what I see

as my car key makes a click.

This is what I'm looking for

and this is what

I
see.

JOURNEYS

I NORTH

This is a particularly
treacherous journey
as it's signposted
exclusively
by question marks.

There's only one exception and it comes in the form
of a vague promise that there may be a destination —
often the most distinguishable star in the sky.
We look towards it as we seek —
for simplicity's sake, let's call it Jerusalem.

With all these question marks it's no wonder we look forward
to each night as a time to shed our clothes and be shrouded
only by the black wings of our dreams —
to sip wine from a pewter chalice with rubies, emeralds and gold.
How beautifully the colors reflect in blue-black and our dreams at night.

But actually, this journey offers little
in the way of encampment and as
the wind slaps cold rain onto our faces,
we have no choice but to move.
It's an enigma wanting to be here at all

and moving forward is an antidote
to such things
as devastation and fear —

so we move on
even farther.

At times the air that we breathe suspends us
and at times it whips us down.
This is why sometimes
we tremble before that
which we love most.

And it makes me wonder, as I pull my hood up over my head
if just before dying – do we breathe
only the ether that's in the air?
And does our blood turn into mercury
as our flesh turns into bone?

II SOUTH

I'm going underground for this one. I carry the Sun
in my eyes and slither into a cave because
I know it can be dark down there.

There's a bright yellow slit where my pupils should be.
You see, the Sun is so strong outside and it's bitten me.
Feeling dizzy, what I really need is to take off my shoes
and potter around barefoot on the basement floor tiles.

I notice the daisies enthusiastically situated on the grass outside.
They watch as I organize family photos and sort laundry.
The four of us are on a bench.
We're little, big, hopeful and smart,
lost and pulled together
two adults and two children -
still so young at heart.

As the telephone rings I breathe in
the stillness of the air.

The ring is muffled by bongo drums
pounding in the park near here
where it feels so safe in the basement
with vibrations so cool
and shaded from the midday sun.

I take a sip of bubbly water
with ice cubes and a splash of grenadine,
watch the bubbles rising...say hello to a friend on the phone.
Many things are growing here right now
in this peaceful place of Earth's darkness underground,
while the daisies outside are exuberantly
infusing my belly with light.

The Sun has slithered into my veins
and never
have I ever felt so alive
as thisssss.

III EAST

There are mainly just memories here. Some
are so distant that it's difficult to say
how this story begins.
What I know is I was given a name that means light
and my surname means dome, as in a celestial cavern.

My middle names reveal an angel and a dragon.
What I've discovered over time is that this picture
of angels, dragons, celestial caverns and light
is a lot to cope with,

so I've developed a taste
for simplicity.
With a good flashlight in hand
I love for directions to be clear.
This is why in my spare time I plant trees.

Just the other day I planted a butterfly tree
which is technically called a Buddleia though I prefer
its nickname, which tells
of its ability to attract endangered insects.

In summer, lizards scamper on the grass
and butterflies flutter around the petals of different lavenders and blue.
Although traditionally it's had a reputation as a "borderline shrub",
the fashion today is to see the dramatic effect
of its tiny petals assembled.

But the butterfly tree is in the middle of this story and the point is
I'm still here with a flashlight looking for what's at the start.
Actually, there's something about how the Sun rose today
that sheds light on this part.

It begins with a lantern and a cave
where angels and dragons are floating.
And behind this, there's something that holds the picture together
which has to do with names and what sets it all in motion.
This is before the beginning.

And this thing that I seek
I've discovered today, is simply a word
that can only mean silence.
This is what's there at the start
and it appears in the darkness before there's the light.

IV WEST

Crack, crack, crack is the sound of my feet
as they walk upon twigs
and swoosh is the sound of a branch I throw past me
whoosh is the sound of the wind
and boom is the sound of a rifle

except that there are no hunters here. We're too close to Paris
and in this part of the forest there are only rabbits and porcupines,
ducks on the lakes, but no longer wild boar or deer.
In any case, for the purposes of this story it doesn't matter what exists —
these being words just blown onto a page.

The only hunting I ever do is at flea markets
where I track floral arrangements and miniature characters
on ceramic tableware, often from Limoges. I also look at the books
and smell their yellowed pages. I'm quite fond of children's stories
with brightly colored illustrations.

Merrily, merrily I amble along and don't always notice
the dream within hours — not more than the rain.
I billow up my red umbrella like a whale that snorts foam into the breeze
and feel safe in that glowing red place that stands up to all menace.
It rains and pours, the old man snores and so on and so forth I dream

though I do know an old man that hunts in this forest.
He's been perched in a tree for years. One day I came to his spot
and asked him straight out why he stays up there shooting all day —
why he shoots with an unloaded rifle and why he aims at invisible deer.
He answered that what he hunts is not the deer themselves.

It's the thought of them he's after — the gentle love in their gaze.
Then he advised me that should danger appear in my neck of the woods
I should stare it straight down — take a bite of a juicy red apple.
He said this turns the Devil himself to black ash and assured me
darkness sometimes drifts sideways, but always ends up falling down.

Back home I clean the dust off a wooden bookcase and think
about what it must feel like to be a good-hearted hunter
perched up in those woods — about Easter eggs with gold wrappings,
swirling kites with rainbow-colored streamers
and the warming sun that sets more and more slowly each day.

And I think about the harvest of spring
about wood, words and wind
about if the hunter
has ever considered
giving red umbrellas to deer.

ROSES

I rarely put on gloves when I tend to them, and even as I look for antiseptic spray, I think more about how to plant and transplant, where to cut and when. In the thorny shadows of my backyard, I always give special care to a rose. For the most part, I use good sense and do pretty much whatever I want, but there are some things I've learned:

- Pruning is best in spring when timed with the first forsythia.
- Make clean cuts at 45-degree angles, exposing the center to light and air.
- Speak to them in French if possible, though any romance language will do.
- They don't like yelling and their taste in music is eclectic.
- Don't over-water. Don't under-water. Don't take them for granted.

To be fair I have to say that though some of them may seem picky, I've found most to be quite modest with their demands even if their utterances do sometimes appear impassioned and bold. In fact, the more I discover, the more I see that thinking about roses is like thinking about love as the entire process is clouded with mystery and driven by hope and desire. They have a reputation for seeming aloof, but for the most part they're not ill-intentioned. Their chatter tends to be no more than polite boasting and is often grounded in facts:

- Cleopatra's palaces were carpeted with rose petals.
- Confucius had over 600 books all about them.
- Secret messages are hidden within each colored bud and flower.

"I'm bursting with love!" exclaims the young red rose.

"Will you love me?" says the timid white.

"Don't you love me anymore?" queries the anxious yellow.

  - The pink one is full of gentle emotions and sweet thoughts.

  - And then there's the unattainable blue rose...

Recently I found myself in the midst of a disagreement between an unassuming, pink rose bush and a fast climbing liana outside my front garden window. The roses had been looking sickly ever since I'd moved into my home and I noticed the liana was furiously making lots of little florets along the banister. As I watched this weed take over, I saw the rose bush become more tired and withered. At first I thought the liana's delicate white petals were attractive, but little by little I realized they were full of malice and were slowly invading the entire front garden space. I was determined to get to the bottom of all the trouble so I spent several hours on different days following sticky green trails that had entwined themselves all around the balcony and down the rose tree into the ground. As the roses gasped for air, I proceeded to slowly disentangle the invading plant.

During the days when I was outside working, a friendly neighbor across the street sometimes came by and we chatted.

  - Lianas are parasites, she told me.

  - They nourish themselves by clinging to other vibrant plants and flowers.

  - The stems are sinuous, snake-like, and hard to get rid of.

It took weeks at different intervals cutting back and probing into the earth to finally get to a point where the liana was managed. While dealing with the garden issue and settling into my new home I got to know most of my neighbors. Little by little, as with all groups, I noticed that there were alliances and tensions that had formed amongst the inhabitants of my block. It was something like what I was observing within my garden.

I learned that my building was constructed on the site of a mansion that had been torn down back in the 1970s to make space for a proper paved road. This house was typical of the bigger twentieth-century trend toward urbanization in this sleepy suburban village. But I also understood that unlike some of the newer constructions that have gone up, our building has its own unique charm as it was an original design and hadn't been promoted by some big anonymous corporation. In fact, the owner himself had participated in the construction and followed building codes without trying to finagle advantages. He kept the number of floors to just three, made only five separate apartments, and preserved most of the surrounding garden. This is how we became the inheritors of the magnificent rose bushes and other trees that surrounded the property, to begin with. We also have five varieties of fruit trees. And by the way, roses, though not considered a fruit tree, do bear fruit and their leaves, buds, and petals are edible.

Over time I've seen how the entire block often turns toward us as a gathering spot for parties, petitions, associations, and other neighborhood events. Most of them never saw the old mansion that was there before and think our building has a discreet sort of cheerful, modern charm. But even with all the friendliness, there are some power dynamics that remind me of the battle of the rose and the liana in my garden. These issues have manifested themselves occasionally at gatherings and particularly a few years ago when we found ourselves fighting the construction of a new building project on the road just behind us.

Previously our little property, with its maple trees at the back, had always also been bordered by a beautiful old farm with an inner courtyard. This had probably been one of the oldest structures in the village, dating back hundreds of years before it got knocked down. It used to be a joy to walk past it every day on the street side at the back. I loved that the flowered courtyard was open to the road for all to see and that the height of the structure was lower than the trees in our backyard. This way we had sunlight in our garden with a warm westerly slant in the evening that was particularly glowing in summer.

But in place of the old farmhouse, promoters built a four-story cement block that the entire neighborhood had fought against. As this company was too mighty for us, we lost the fight to stop the construction altogether, though we did win on certain points. During the battle, people bickered about some members of the association not pulling their weight or only fighting for specific issues that concerned them directly without tackling the issue as a whole. There was a lot of finger-pointing and disrespect, and mainly I noticed a sinuous creeping need on the part of some to take control. I remember thinking this is how sweet-tempered pink roses end up getting bullied and then wither.

Although since then things have calmed down between the rose and the liana, I've come to realize that this is a struggle that will never end. It's part of an ancient war between might and right, evil and good, beauty and vileness that goes on all the time and the battleground is everywhere, in one form or another, and even in my own head. So I'm glad the Liana retreated and that we managed to get the promoters of the ugly building to scale back to four floors instead of six and to make green space on balconies.

Today with the construction finished, we're still able to have dinners in our backyard and the community is, for the most part, back to its old convivial ways. So I suppose for the time being there's been some sort of victory - at least until someone else decides to sell, and then knock down and build on another side. Coming back to roses, however, I'd like to add a few items to the things I've learned:

- The way into the garden is through the narrow gate as there isn't much room for weeds and self-serving climbers.
- The gateway is surrounded by all kinds of roses, each deserving consideration from the others.
- Dinner parties with french cheese and wine usually work great, but good cheer is key.
- Love your neighbor as yourself, or at least try to.
- Weed out all that stuff that just drags you down.

Like the variants of love that each of us may feel in time, every rose tells a different story about the awakening of the self into the divine — their scents alone tell of their truest natures. And yes, the thorns may warn of adversity, but the flowers themselves make us dream: the candlelit encounter, the weekend cottage by the sea, and the simplest impromptu affirmation of love that arrives in the form of a dazzling bouquet.

"Et Marion les roses, les roses font un beau bouquet

Les roses font un beau bouquet, quand elles sont jolies"

This means that roses make a magnificent bouquet especially when every one of them is lovely. This is true. We are often mysteries even to ourselves. But I can say with utter conviction that I love all roses and particularly the luscious dark red ones. I recently received a magnificent bouquet of these.

I watched them go from budding to full bloom, and thought...

Indeed they are so lovely...

PART III

BY THE WATERSIDE

THE BASKET

There's a basket in this house. It's there on the wooden table
in the living room by the stove, on the bed with puffy pillows
or the kitchen countertop. It's there before it gets tossed
into the backseat of the car, carried away and dragged about
with its wicker reed stitching on edges that fray with years
and patterns that almost disappear, though far less
than the content of what's held within — as this is a secret

What's apparent is the circular weave whose numbers
both change and persist with alternate evens and odds,
fastening shape, not perfectly round but the sum of its own circularity,
and this too is a secret like the principles of polyhedra
with golden and other rainbow-colored rules

The truth is found in the 3's and the 5's, the 12's and 30's
as they act out their roles and soliloquize about the friendliness
of horizontal planes — about how the spiral is a baseline
from which the harmony grows

But talk of emotion would clutter the basket as it speaks more of light
shows ways, casts shadows, that alter the hues of the reds,
blues and whites

How they hold on to each other
while carrying on —

they carry on

with the question of identity being irrelevant to them as they do
what they do — they contain

And while sometimes the basket seems empty
it also sometimes seems full, depending
on the day or the weather, the light from the Moon—

the thought of the basket sometimes yields pain —
the opulent hollowness there in the faces, the peeks, the stops,
the loops and the song of icy weather when it floats from limbo
to alcove and bay with an insipid pallor that permeates the day,

and of warmer months when the chill has passed and it stands
copious and tall —a cornucopia of brightly colored fruit hangs
from its rim, brings emptiness to fullness, makes all things lush again,
as even when it's just half full, something precious lays dormant where
a hearthside dream's entwined within and tucked away with care

There's a basket in this house — it's part empty and part full
with what comes from me and from my mother,
her mother and before — hands clasped round
and carrying from cave to crib into the grave
the festive treats both reeped and found from gardens
to markets and squares, to houses built with two by fours
and driveways, split level byways and trails
from mother to daughter, the secret moves round
from mother to daughter — goes round

THE STORM

The story takes place in what can only be called a dark
and stormy night in a wooded suburb near Paris.

*****

During the day there had been such heat and humidity that even
the idea of going for a swim had become unappealing. I remember staying
inside shades drawn, looking at pictures of modern houses made of wood
and glass in an architectural magazine. I was thinking about the vibrancy of
these materials; their solidity, transparency, the light that shifts with the
seasons, and times of day — about how our bodies are like houses, how we
adapt to our environment and how adapting, we change.

That day I saw that a spider had woven a very big web.

*****

Meanwhile, on the other side of the forest, my good friend Pat was not at
all at home with the shades drawn, but inside someone else's house. She was
listening to a sad family saga unraveling itself so as to shake the very
foundations upon which their lives had been made. She told me that she had
learned that a small river was flowing far beneath the ground — that there
was humidity in the basement from overflowing springs. She said she
believed it was the energy from the river that had divided the home. That
same afternoon she performed a ritual with salt that she drizzled into various
pockets all around the house, leaving a faint but gleaming trail.

I remember listening to her and thinking "how interesting, how bizarre..."

That night as I lay in bed sleeping, there was a roar of thunder that made the entire forest shake. Rain poured down in torrents, shutters knocked themselves about, windows blew open and doors slammed shut. Every time I fell asleep another waft of wind would escape from a window, cutting through what had been the dense catatonia of our afternoon. Between bouts of sleep, I thought about vibrations in a household, about my own family, the planet, and about the spider that had woven its web.

*****

I woke up the next day with an odd image of Ariadne, the Greek goddess whose magical thread had guided the hero Theseus down into the darkest reaches of the minotaur's den and then guided his escape back out again.

The initial picture was of Ariadne lying on the beach of Naxos, the island where she had just been abandoned by her lover Theseus. She was dressed in an orange silk gown and was inert, like a sleeping beauty in a Pre-Raphaelite painting. I imagined Theseus depositing her on the beach, thinking she must be dead from the tossing and turning of their boat throughout the stormy night before.

Traditionally, there are two versions of the story. There's the dark version that has Theseus abandon Ariadne, even after all she has done for him. She wakes up and then tragically kills herself by hanging on the thread. But there's another bright version that has her sailing off with Dionysus, the God of the harvest, festivities, laughter, and wine.

In my half-sleep, I imagined my own joyous version which has Ariadne feign sleep precisely so that Theseus will go away. He, powerful, but not a deep thinker or emotionally very mature, deposits her onto the shore with no more than a dim feeling of remorse before blithely moving on to his future adventures which, amongst other things, will include the founding of the city of Athens.

Meanwhile, she serenely winds up the thread which is now encrusted with multicolored bangles, beads and jewels gathered from all the layers of rock, salt and silt along the journey down through the maze below. She smiles as she remembers Daedelus, the wise old man who had initially empowered her with the trick of the thread. And then she watches Theseus recede into the yonder as Dionysus emerges on the sunlit horizon of the warm and breezy late June morning sea.

My Ariadne would never hang herself on the string after Theseus leaves. And she would necessarily contrive to get that dull-witted jock turned politician to go on without her. She would then joyously sail off with Dionysus, the infinitely more appealing former folk/rock star turned organic wine farmer.

I could so easily picture Ariadne and Dionysus living happily ever after on an ecologically sustainable vineyard in the Mediterranean surrounded by children and friends and having fun parties with luscious food, wine, music and dancing. She would write poetry in her spare time – one poem for each bangle she'd collected on her string.

Later that morning, I thought about how sometimes things happen in sequences that elude us, and sometimes, like Ariadne, we forge the patterns ourselves.

It begins with photosynthesis and then there's a woven web — baby spiders crawling about.

*****

Spiders have eight legs; four for the directions, and four for the winds. It's believed that the hinges of their webs are invisible letters that are as instructive as they are insignificant. I bet that if asked they could write novels about their point of view on things such as storms. And I'm certain they know more than we about diligence, perseverance, fatality and conviction. They certainly don't seem to be of the kind that give up easily. I suppose it helps if you've got eight arms and legs.

As I bailed water out of the garage the day after the storm, I considered the size of the spider I had seen the day before. I thought how I would hate to be caught in a web and how clever Ariadne was at spinning dreams out of misfortune. I wondered how much I could ever really know about the goings on of that, or any day.

Sometimes I feel I know too much and sometimes too little.
Sometimes I just want to escape.
Sometimes I want to linger and learn with the telling.
And sometimes ...

I wonder how much is simply there between claps of thunder in the night, plain as day, in the middle of the dream.

THE CYPRESS TREES

*He built the house near the cypress trees in the shadows
and that's where she'd gone to stay.
During the days they took the livestock to pasture
and during the nights they made a fire, ate soup and then lay.*

It was a peaceful life but for the shadows, which they lit with hopes and sweet dreams. And it was only over time that disquiet crept into the darkness, and made all that peace disappear

For days and days the rain poured, and for nights and nights the wind shrieked, and then she realized that it rained even when the sun shone, that the shriek was heard dead through the night, that the stir had swarmed into her heart's core and that peace could be found there no more. So she went out the door...and was gone.

Though they say it's misguided to think the grass may be greener elsewhere, it's worse to just sit where the grass has turned brown. But this story is not really about valleys and shepherds. It takes place in a little suburban town outside of Paris.

The house was not built by the man in the story, but by someone else sometime between the first and second world wars, at a time when the town was developing from a country village into a major industrial suburb. The man in this story worked in home renovation and the woman with the local public schools. There were children, and occasionally they'd take care of a neighbor's dog. When they ate soup, it was not by the fire but by the TV, and dinner was often accompanied by treats from the local supermarket like little inexpensive cheeses and wine.

47

The harmony that had reigned in that home was disturbed not by the shadows themselves, but by the man and woman's very different ways of coping with them. She would often hover in mid-range making lots of delicate side-steps, seeing adversity as a kind of bizarre challenge, feeling dreary and perplexed. Whereas he would surge out to the limit and then retreat into seclusion, bolting the shutters, locking the doors, cursing the world and then festering in suspicion.

There's no question that people can have very different ways of coping with duress. The differences are not so much in courage but in how the temperaments play out. They both wanted to repair what had busted apart. But paradoxically, of the two she was both the dreamer and the realist. Just as he would taunt her to remain with him stuck in the mire, she would respond by looking at him despairingly while on a deeper level she'd be searching for clues as to how to get out of the muddle.

At the time of the drama, she saw that if just one of them always dreamed into darkness then they would both end up with no more than a pain-filled penumbra of what had been that initial enchantment. The cold, harsh twist came with the fact that he found a strange satisfaction in imagining gloomy and disaster-filled endings. At first the pattern of darkness was just a vague undercurrent, but little by little it took root and grafted itself more and more firmly under their skins. She felt the destruction was linked to the man's father who had often called his son worthless as a child. And though his mother seemed kind, she had probably been the type that always played the victim, feeling overwhelmed.

Over time, the woman's patience for all of this misery dulled and she began to understand these details with little more than clinical detachment.

There was a shotgun the man kept in the closet that he took from his father when he had died. Was it the gun his father had killed himself with? She never asked – she didn't want to know. It looked old. Did it date back to the war? And why the whiskey bottle would come out with every full moon, along with abusive language – this too, she had ceased to care. He would tell her to close the car door more gently...stop using hyperbole to make a point clear... never ever serve mustard along with roast lamb – so much pointless intermittent howling. Werewolf. But she had her children's futures to consider. So, this is when the hard realism kicked in – at least for her it did. She realized soon enough that this man was too busy stuck in the corner licking his own wounds.

 But this story
is not about werewolves or monsters
or demons as some might think or say,
but more about weather and tillage conditions,
and how to make the valley green again one day.

In France, after the occupation, people didn't just shut their homes and steal away incognito to somewhere else. And they didn't retreat inwards either and harken back to better times. There were no better times. The First World War alone had left almost 1.5 million French soldiers dead. So at the end of the Second World War what many people did was to regroup in Paris where the modern world would quickly rush forward and bring things into a new and very different focus. There was a kind of unspoken pact the country had made not to dwell on the past. But perhaps they had also tried too hard to forget. Perhaps that's part of the reason why the shadows like termites were left crawling throughout the beams of their homes and even into this house.

It would be difficult to judge what the right distance might be between us and ourselves - how much to heed those second thoughts that keep lurking in the bigger story with its older pattern of lies and deceit. There had been fingers that scratched for edible roots down in the ground, neighbors that denounced one another and shadows that projected themselves even here now, into this story with cypress trees. So much darkness would come to haunt the bushes and doorways — that would leave the next generations feeling never good enough to merit being loved.

If there was a consolation it came in the byways lined with Cypress trees. It was as if they formed a map of their own resilience, indicating the distance traveled and the way forward by sheer steadfastness. And over time she too would notice how the tree grows branches parallel to its trunk. She would admire how the branches point upward toward the sky with aspiration, how they never stray far from the core and how they tend more toward allegiance than adventure.

This is all to explain that while the grass may seem greener on the other side of the mountain, a simple shift to another pasture along the same slope can sometimes do just fine —

to make subtle **adjustments** in functioning
open new doors and close others

to operate a change of perspective

refreshing

as a stroll

on a nearby hill

is more like what **the woman**

in this story

would manage

with the help of courage

and sheer will

No scratching at wounds with blood covered claws. No wrenching of hands or shotguns sounding off at all hours of the night. No, no, no...that was the stuff of cheap drama for people that lack imagination, or so she thought amidst all the commotion, even then. In any case, she was too busy climbing mountains in her own backyard to waste time making yet more of a mess. She kissed him goodbye before going. He stared off into space, stood tall and said nothing. Resilience.

As she left that house she thought if she should die on her way to the new house, she would wish to be buried near a cypress tree by a spring, where wildflowers might grow. But for now she would go to a pasture that was a bit more green just a few doors down the road.

It was a cottage whose lawn at springtime would be overgrown with daffodils and crocuses swaying joyfully in the wind. Her children would come home each day with drawings to put on the refrigerator door, seedlings to plant in the garden and friends to play with after school. With the neighbors they'd exchange apples in October and apricots in July, roses and lilac bunches of pinks and lavenders and blues. She would find new companionship, new love and new trails to walk along in the forest. She would sometimes think about the Cypress trees ever-growing nearby.

as yes, it would be peaceful and sunny there
wherever she might someday lay.
With that thought she closed the door
... and then she went away.

SECRET GARDENS

I   SEEDS

It's about reaping and sowing. Planting comes with an incantation:
Earth, Water, Sun, Air, and so forth...
But if they take root and manage to survive the stray weeds
and whatnot that lingers
they become more like prophecies.
Some of the older surrounding ones may not always
be helpful, as their thick and twisted roots
can make the newer ones lack air.
And this is where the shears, the trowel and twine come in.
It's difficult to make choices.
Small roots and vines are one thing
but it's criminal to fell a tree that's still bursting with life.

At least evergreens are persistent and don't beg questions
in quite the same way.
It takes sobriety to spring forth from rock.
And they're relentless in how they cope
with rain, heat, cold, unfriendly neighbors,
everybody, everything and all at once – relentless
with those needles they've got for leaves
that pierce through the Sun
and carry back its vigor.

Daffodils are not relentless,
but they do stand up to storms at night.
There's strength in the way they know how
to have fun amongst themselves.
Crocuses are more varied in color, but smaller.

Lilies are more delicate but white.
Call them all what you will, it's downright wrong
to revile innocence.
They don't require much in the way of care, and
their whispered invitations
carry so much more meaning
then one might think.

Thankfully, in this picture there is also a flowering tree —
delicate, mesmerizing, ephemeral,
but in a very constant sort of way.
Just look at the lilac, there is no dilettantism here.
The petals always falling and opening, yet rooted —
concentric waves of perpetual ceremony
that takes the breath away.

But, sometimes it's difficult to know how to look, to listen,
to strike the right balance,
to respect, forgive and create limits while fostering growth.
Dirt tends to accumulate under one's nails
and perhaps, it's enough just to be grateful
for the chance to reap and sow at all —
each of us in our own ways...
Earth, Water, Sun, Air and so forth...
The words alone can be a challenge.

II THE BIRCH TREE

This is the path. This is the pebble.
This is the shoe. This is the foot.
And this is the Moon, by day — a ray of the most crystalline light

shining all along this path...and we have stopped walking.
It wasn't necessary for there to have been so much pain.
No stumble, no fall — just a sharpness
right in the sole of a small boy's foot.

Sometimes the suspension is dense. It shrinks inwards
before it glistens like the pebbles along this path. In this place,
the spectrum of the Earth's darkness
reflects myriad shadings of white.
But just now the perspective is narrowed —
pressed right onto the point
where that pebble is being taken out of the shoe.
Small fingers hold and shake out all of what's there:
sharpness, fragmentation, dissonance.
Real chaos is such that it can engender only respite.

The silence is disturbed by the rustle of leaves
and the distant murmur of cars that pass along the street below.
The late afternoon moon is witness to this smallest of rituals.
Her enigmatic gaze resonates with the leaves of a birch tree
as if discoursing about something that has not yet occurred.
So delicate the leaves respond in agreement and shimmer
in a way that looks like so many small mirrors
casting reflections each upon the other.
Actually, they seem to be smiling, and then the wind alights.
It blows even into the hollow parts of the trunk
of this most solid tree.

And it feels as though another root has extended itself
even into this small place.
Only a few adjustments need somehow to be made.
But with the shoe back on
we smile and hold hands and move forwards.

III THE TRELLIS

Steady and sure, although there is fragility there, as there always is.
Call the others surrounding what you will; wild rose,
dogwood, wisteria.
Betwixt and between, they all do manage to get into your grain.
I think I know what they're climbing for.
At least I have an intuition that somehow we're all the same.
The sound of a motorcycle far away in the middle of the night
both reassures and frightens.
Comfort and fear — No fools are we.

And there you are climbing up to the top of those, your very stairs.
Step by step you move upwards and step by step with each
season you hang on and you stumble and even you may fall.
The trick is to clip the stems when the flowers are faded.
The other trick is water, and of course sunlight,
and to sing, dance and pray — as we have always done each day.

You are now both going up and going down.
You look, you listen and you move. And then back upwards.
Up the crossovers and up onto where the vertical and horizontal
meet and then go far beyond.
It's the smell of the wild grass that lingers on.
And do consider the diagonal paths that cover more ground
and are sturdy.

Wherever a nail is driven into a piece of wood
the past and the present come together.
That's what fixes it in time.
One step, two steps, three steps up — with that strength
to take you further
upwards, downwards, across.

One day you will shed the faded flowers
and enjoy the new ones growing by themselves.
A force is at work here that we do not fully understand.
Sometimes that force actually reaches and pulls up.
And another step may always appear. The trick is to see it.
The trick is to make it make another up and up.
It's not so bad to look down. Look down and smile.
Go down and look.
Go up climbing and see. Look at that horizon.
Even the birds passing in the sky will tell you to remember –
take with you only what is good.

THE RIVER

It's about time — about this river whose tree-lined banks we've ambled along with its barges, buildings and bridges. It's about seagulls flying in deft alignment along its corridor in spring, and about the song that an accordionist plays here, along this same river as it ripples and flows. There's something nostalgic in the shifting muddy waters of a river — something of memory and change, and right now.

History is one thing. It begins long ago in the Bronze Age with Gaul settlements in earthen huts, and flows past Notre Dame, The Louvre, The Eiffel Tower. It begins at its source in the Alps and flows into an estuary at the Channel between England and France. From its banks, we carry back many things which like the skins of fish are discarded though beautiful.

And then there's memory. The original settlers recorded their world in a prism of trees. They had a secret language called Ogham which was spoken using fingers as letters to communicate about the body and the seasons.

We are constantly retrieving odd things from the past as we amble along with the persistent river's flow. We dive down into the silt with our thoughts and then emerge as if to align them like the lindens and poplars and planes along the Seine. This is what we're doing when we journey down to these banks. And one thing always leads to another.

The sound of a siren, a foghorn, an accordion, even the rustle of leaves is evocative here. And this is where history and memory briefly disconnect and re-combine in the feeling of what's present. Just now, as the accordion plays, it makes less of a picture than an impression.

It's a community dance on the banks of the Seine, just after the Second World War, in late spring. Lanterns are strung around a linden tree. There are tables and chairs and many people of all ages dancing. There's an ambiance of gaiety that affirms itself with their steps on the post-war gravel beneath their feet. A man and a woman are gazing into each other's eyes. They share the same glass of wine. They're dressed-up, though simply. She wears a red dress with a delicate floral pattern. Her sandals are high-heeled but worn. He wears a white shirt that's tucked into his trousers with a belt. The shirt is slightly wrinkled and the cuffs are rolled up. They're young and look into one another's eyes with such desire that everything else recedes into a lantern-lit haze.

This is the picture, although the exact time and place are impossible to recall. I know it's somewhere by the river and I try to imagine who the man and woman are. The look in her eyes is so familiar that I wonder if she couldn't be me. The feeling is such that I'm not sure if it's a memory or a wish. And the accordion plays...

"Ce dont je me souviens c'est qu'ils étaient heureux les yeux au fond des yeux et c'était bien... yes, it was good..."

THE CEDAR TREE

There are several stories in this story.
This is typical of cedars.
The roots tell of branches
which tell of shadows

which tell of light
and magic and seasons and ordinary people passing
telling stories of the storytelling cedar tree
as I do now with this one in France.

There was once a grand vizier
who came from the east with a gift
opulent and sensual, scented, oriental
ornate and fundamental as gold
frankincense, myrrh - a grand and little thing
to make a stir.
What else would one give to a king?

But it really began
with a botanist - Bernard de Jussieu
who wore them in his hat one day
after stumbling and breaking pots
on his way to a ceremonious reverence
to the king with pirouette, alouette, gentille lark
whistling a winsome tune to sun and moon

and back again
as not long after more cedar trees would grow
planted by a woman for her husband, the floral painter
Redouté — one tree each day as children were born

with roots and branches knitting the years and yawning
this diddy of the painter, the woman
the cedars growing and the city

where gentlefolk and merry pranksters
still poke round here now
with talk that travels back to Jerusalem, the temple,
Noah, the ark, paper scrolls made of bark, before
we could read or had heard anyone say a word
about the wheel, the worship of idols, pots and pans
the uses of clay

Gilgamesh — in cuneiform script on tablets,
sword in hand roams the land,
combats shadow, light, frost, twists, turns, and snow
before he penetrates the forest door of Ishtar,
Mother of the Kish, Uruk, Ur,
realizing anyone can die from a snakebite:
the poison or simply the wound

anyone — though we can now count to ten
make digital prints of back then
and me, for example, here on the branch of this mighty tree
watching children explore the contours and height,
languishing as I do in the dappled
late afternoon light.
This too is worth recounting.

As an old French dictum says:
"The greater the tree, the greater its shadow."
This alone tells ...
quite a lot.

ABOUT THE AUTHOR
LUCIA COPPOLA

Lucia Coppola is an ESL (English Second Language) teacher who is originally from New York and has lived in France and California. She has a professional background in dance and body techniques. Her writing is informed by nature and traditional storytelling. Some of her work has been read on the Clocktower New River Writers radio and published with Inspirelle, The Parliament, Vita Brevis, Soul-Lit, Songs of Eretz, Adelaide and Plants and Poetry.

ABOUT THE PUBLISHER
PLANTS & POETRY

Plants & Poetry is a small, women and indigenous-owned business founded in Northwest Arkansas in 2019. Cofounders, Jamie Nix and Leslie Walker create a space that nurtures a love for the arts and science, offering poetry & plant education to reconnect with the soil and soul.

Leslie Walker manages a Food Forest, The Oasis, in Bella Vista, where she hosts various workshops and events. Jamie Nix operates a nature-inspired publication, *Plants & Poetry Journal*. For every submission received at the Journal, they plant a tree or type of vegetation in The Oasis. Plants & Poetry Journal publishes poetry, prose, mixed media, and creative nonfiction.

CPSIA information can be obtained
at www.ICGtesting.com
Printed in the USA
BVHW090008190822
644959BV00002B/7

9 798886 801675